UNDER HIS SHADOW

WRITINGS
Volume 2

by David Mayorga

Published by

SHABAR PUBLICATIONS
www.shabarpublications.com

Most Shabar Publications products are available at special quantity discounts for bulk purchase for sales promotions, fund-raising and educational needs. For details, write Shabar Publications at mayorga1126@gmail.com.

Under His Shadow Writings Volume 2 *by David Mayorga*
Published by Shabar Publications
3833 N. Taylor Rd.
Palmhurst, Texas 78573
www.shabarpublications.com
www.masterbuildertx.com

This book or parts thereof may not be reproduced in any form, stored in a retrieval system, or transmitted in any form by any means - electronic, mechanical, photocopy, recording, or otherwise - without prior written permission of the publisher, except as provided by United States of America copyright law.

Unless otherwise noted, all Scripture quotations are from the New Kings James Version of the Bible. Copyright@1979, 1980, 1982 by Thomas Nelson, Inc., publishers. Used by permission.

Edited by Emily Rose King

Copyright @ 2021 by David Mayorga

All rights reserved

ISBN 978-1-955433-02-0

Table of Contents

Introduction 5
Day 1: No Matter What - Don't Lose Heart! 7
Day 2: Renewed Day by Day! 11
Day 3: Realizing Our Life Is No Longer Ours! 15
Day 4: Holy Ghost Adrenaline! 19
Day 5: Christ's Appeal:
        On Becoming God's Salesman! 23
Day 6: Having Nothing and Yet Possessing All Things!... 27
Day 7: It's Time to Step It Up! 31
Day 8: Don't Be a Stupid Fellow! 35
Day 9: For Your Sakes! 39
Day 10: The Cross Test! 43
Day 11: It Seems Right! 46
Day 12: Giving from the Heart! 49
Day 13: Lending to the Lord! 53
Day 14: We are God's Habitation! 56
Day 15: Discerning the Works of Darkness! 60
Day 16: Disciplined Lifestyle! 64
Day 17: Excuses, Excuses, Excuses! 67
Day 18: Don't Set Your Eyes on What is Not! 71
Day 19: Exalted Above Measure? 75

Day 20: You Have to Know Your Place! 79
Day 21: Build It Twice! 83
Day 22: What Is Tying You Down? 86
Day 23: On Being Complete 90
Day 24: Communion of the Holy Spirit! 94
Day 25: Are You Responsible for the Assignment? 98
Day 26: Man-Pleasers! 102
Day 27: On Being Patient 106
Day 28: The Beauty of Arabia! 109
Day 29: Until I Am Satisfied! 113
Day 30: The Life Which I Now Live! 117
Day 31: The Deceit of Charm and Beauty! 121
Day 32: It Is All Vanity! 125
Day 33: The Tudor! 129
Day 34: Until Christ Is Formed! 132
Day 35: When the Honeymoon Is Over! 136
Day 36: It Will be Well! 140
Day 37: With All Your Might! 144
Day 38: Recognize Yourself! 148
Day 39: Learning to Sow Continually! 152
Day 40: Man's Initial Calling! 155
Ministry Resources 159
Ministry Information 160

Introduction

"Awake, O north wind,
And come, O south!
Blow upon my garden,
That its spices may flow out." (Song of Solomon 4:16)

After writing my first volume, Under His ShadowWritings, I felt inspired by the Holy Spirit to continue developing material that came out of times of prayer and fasting.

I don't mean to sound like a spiritual guru, mystical or different, but let me just say that there are thoughts and revelations that God gives His servants at different times of their lives for various reasons.

I truly and deeply feel like a garden before the Lord. I made Song of Solomon 4:16 my prayer. **"Awake, o north wind and come o south! Blow upon my garden, that its spices may flow out."**

I had a desire to go deeper with God, and so I set my heart and mind to fast for forty days and nights in the last season. My experience with God was incredible, so much so that I have more earnestly adopted a life of prayer and fasting.

Out of my quiet times, I noticed that the Lord started to share some interesting things with me. This is one of the reasons that I decided to continue writing during times of fasting and prayer; and this is truly how the idea of writing these volumes was born.

I am writing a series of volumes called Under His Shadow—Writings, in order to communicate what the Spirit of God is prophetically saying to me during these times of separation and consecration through fasting and prayer, is truly the goal and mission of these writings.

May your heart be enriched, and may the Lord empower you in your inner-man, as you yearn for a greater touch of God in your own life!

David Mayorga, *Author*
McAllen, Texas

Day 1

No Matter What — Don't Lose Heart!

"Therefore, we do not lose heart. Even though our outward man is perishing, yet the inward man is being renewed day by day." (2 Corinthians 4:16a)

Let me begin my writings by saying that losing heart is a common thing that happens to all believers. You and I will lose heart at various times, yes, we will be disheartened by many outward things that we will face. My friends, this is reality!

What do we do when we are faced with this situation in our lives— when all we see is darkness, loneliness, and the awful feeling of despair? I'm sure that many thoughts have crossed our minds during these dark moments.

I believe that afflictions do come, and when they come, we must be able to ask ourselves the right questions before rebuking people, situations and even the devil himself! It is such a natural tendency to quickly rebuke all that is negative without giving it much thought. When pain comes, all we can think about is simply surviving it.

Believe me, I understand you. I get it! I have been in this place where all I want is for the pain to go away and to just disappear! I think that this is the main reason why believers embrace a doctrine of painlessness and prosperity. It is not that I like pain, but I want to see the face of Jesus while in the midst of the fire!

Jesus said, "If anyone comes to Me, and does not hate his own father and mother and wife and children and brothers and sisters, yes, and even his own life [in the sense of indifference to or relative disregard for them in comparison with his attitude toward God]—**he cannot be My disciple."** (Luke 14:26. AMP)

When facing affliction, remember, God is shaping our lives into His likeness. It is not what you and I want; It is always what He desires for us!

I have discovered a secret to overcoming some of life's most crucial moments— let me share it with you.

When you are facing adversity, a challenge, a test, or trial — before you act in any way, take time to seek the face of God. Here's what you ask the Holy Spirit, Why is this situation upon me? Be honest with God. If there is sin in your life, this is your time to confess. Run to the mercy seat!

Now, if there is no known sin that you are committing, conclude that God is developing some much-needed work in your life and character.

Time to Sit Under His Shadow and Learn!

1. Have you ever been disheartened? Share your experience with the group.

2. During your time of losing heart, what actions did you take to stay in tune with God?

3. Did you ever wonder if you were going to make it? Did you doubt God in all your suffering? Be honest with the group and share?

4. Sometimes God will put everything you are wanting to do on hold. Have you ever experienced this? These times of waiting teach us patience and diligence. Share with the

group the last time God allowed this to happen in your life.

5. When being tested and tried, don't be afraid to ask God why He has allowed this situation in your life. The answer might surprise you! Has God ever shared with you why certain experiences took place in your life? Share this with the group.

Day 2

Renewed Day by Day!

"Even though our outward man is perishing, yet the inward man is being renewed day by day." (2 Corinthians 4:16b)

I have often wondered about this verse and how the Apostle Paul made this statement with such authority.

Paul's statement has been life-changing for me.

The Apostle Paul was a man of God. He believed to be called by God for the work of an apostle. He planted churches, established workers, and faced many trials during his service unto God.

I could not speak like Paul, for I would be a fool. But Paul could speak with such authority over what it meant to **"not lose heart."** He could with convincing authority and power say, **"...though our outward man is perishing, yet the in-**

ward man is being renewed..."

It is true that based upon all the challenges he and his apostolic team experienced, they were outwardly perishing. Yet, in the same breath Paul said, **"...the inward man is being renewed day by day."**

How Do We BecomeRenewed Day by Day?

You and I will always and forever be on probation by the Holy Spirit; we will daily be challenged to grow and mature into the fullness of Christ. So how do we stay sane in our endeavor to please God with all that He has given us?

Here's what I have discovered when it comes to renewing ourselves in God:

First, renewal begins with the understanding that we need to be renewed in the life of God. How do we do this? One must come to God and say, *"Lord, I am dust. If you don't pour out your water, (the Holy Spirit) I will remain unchanged in form. I need you to flood me with your Spirit. Let the rivers flow out of me today."* Amen.

Secondly, we must acknowledge that we are perishing due to

age not to mention that our bodies are wasting away slowly. To this we say, *"Thank you God for allowing me to serve you with this decaying body. Yet, it is not by might, not by power, but by Your Spirit that I serve you. Come and flood me like rain again today!"* Amen.

Renewal day by day must be intentional. We must seek God daily for renewal. Renewal might begin on a Sunday morning service or some special prayer meeting, but it must be cultivated and maintained by daily practice!

Time to Sit Under His Shadow and Learn!

1. Have you ever read portions of Scripture that penetrated so deep into the spiritual marrow of your bone that they produced powerful change in you? Share your experience with the group.

2. **"...though the outward man is perishing..."** What does this mean to you? Discuss this with your group.

3. Renewed day by day is a practical way to reignite your fire for God. Have you experienced coldness, indifference, or backsliding in your walk with the Lord?

4. If you have fallen from the place where God placed you, how did you get back? Share with the group.

5. In the devotion above, there is a line that reads: "Renewal day by day must be intentional." What does this mean to you? Share this with the group and see if anyone needs to renew their hearts for God today.

Day 3

Realizing Our Life Is No Longer Ours!

"And He died for all, that those who live should live no longer for themselves, but for Him who died for them and rose again." (2 Corinthians 5:15)

Living out this life that God gave us without the knowledge that we were created by God and for God, can be a very lonely road in life. Making the daily effort to make something out of life without God is hard work.

I have often wondered about people who work 8 to 10 hours a day — what would they be doing if they didn't have this job? Where would they be spending their time and effort? Do you think that you would be asleep and hoping that time would fly by until you see your next television program? Would you spend it leisurely? Would you spend it in depression?

When you don't know what you don't know, it can be a very

depressing emotional ride!

Now, if we realize that Christ has died for us, at least now we can venture out and discover why He did this act of kindness and mercy.

In ourselves, we are limited to knowing the will of God.

Now, if we enter His life, we will discover our destiny. You see, living for us (ourselves) is really a limited way of seeing and living life. When we discover that Christ died for all of us so that we may truly live — then we begin to see our future unfold.

The Scripture says, "that those who live should live no longer for themselves, but for Him who died for them and rose again."

No Longer for Themselves!

The will of God begins when we understand that we are to no longer live for ourselves, but for Him! All of God's plans are set in motion when this decision is made. There may have been many things happening in our life up to this very point, but it's not until our knowledge and understanding of why God died for us increases, that our life begins to take shape – God's way!

It is time to realize that through the cross of Christ, God opened a door for us to enter. Those who have entered have begun to see what life and living are all about! The Scripture says, **"In Him was life, and the life was the light of men."** (John 1:4)

It's time to start living for Him!

Time to Sit Under His Shadow and Learn!

1. Have you ever wondered why Christ died for you? Was it just to be saved or is there something much deeper than that? Discuss this point with the group.

2. For some, a job makes them happy, yet for others, a job is hard work. Many work to get away from home, while others work to pay their bills. Why do you work? Discuss this point with the group.

3. Is your life a joyful one? Why or why not? Share and discuss with the group.

4. The Scripture in 2 Corinthians 5:15 makes a bold statement regarding living out your life for God. Have you embraced what Christ has done for you and are you following His will for your life? Share your own experience with the group.

5. The Scripture in John 1:4 says that "in Him was life." Do you believe in your heart that you have entered this life and are now living out His destiny? Share with the group.

Day 4

Holy Ghost Adrenaline!

"But we have this treasure in earthen vessels, that the excellence of the power may be of God and not of us." (2 Corinthians 4:7)

As we learn to yield in greater fullness to the Lord or surrender our lives to a greater degree, we will begin to experience greater revelations of our purpose in God's assignment for us.

While I was spending some time in prayer and in fasting today, I heard the Lord speak to me so clearly in this Scripture in 2 Corinthians 4:7. I heard the Lord ask me a question and say, David, do you believe that I can use you to have a great impact in the world?

While I meditated upon these words, I had to pay closer attention to what God was really saying to me. I responded to the Lord, Of course I believe that you can use my life for greater impact!

To my response the Lord said, You must know the number one key that I require for greater impact.

What is it Lord? I asked.

The Lord told me, You must know that everything I do in you is by My power, not yours!

Not by Might nor by Power, But by the Holy Spirit!

Often, I have heard these words, but never really paid much attention to what this actually means. Here's what I believe the Lord wants us to understand:

The power of God is released to us by His Spirit that lives within. His Spirit vivifies and quickens our mortal flesh. It releases into our spiritual bloodstream, confidence, faith, and the will to act upon what we have been shown! It's like adrenaline in our bodies, except in a spiritual sense.

What is adrenaline?

It's a hormone secreted by the adrenal glands, especially in conditions of stress, increasing rates of blood circulation, breathing, and carbohydrate metabolism and preparing muscles for exertion. You don't have to press a switch, the body just reacts to it and it happens!

What adrenaline does to your body?

Key actions of adrenaline include increasing the heart rate, increasing blood pressure, expanding the air passages of the lungs, enlarging the pupil in the eye, redistributing blood to the muscles, and altering the body's metabolism, to maximize blood glucose levels (primarily for the brain).

It's almost like becoming a superhuman when this happens to us. Have you experienced this in your own life?

Well, in the spiritual sense, it is the same thing — we are quickened and altered by the Holy Spirit to do great exploits.

We must always remember this: the Lord's desire is that we acknowledge Him at work in us and through us!

Time to Sit Under His Shadow and Learn!

1. The idea of receiving an assignment comes from God.

It is through His Holy Spirit that God's work is to be accomplished. Discuss with your group on the assignment that God has given you and have others share their assignments as well.

2. God takes our human ability and then alters it by His Spirit. Has God called you to do a special task that you felt you were not ready for? Share with the group.

3. Have you been in a place where you felt that if God didn't appear, you would fail? Share with the group.

4. In the Scripture, "that the power may be of God and not of us," means what to you? Discuss the different views with your group.

5. Are you ready for God to release this power in you? Go around the group and ask who is ready for God's hand to be upon them for service. Pray one for another with this thought in mind.

Day 5

Christ's Appeal: On Becoming God's Salesman!

"So, we are Christ's ambassadors, God making His appeal as it were through us. We (as Christ's personal representatives) beg you for His sake to lay hold of the divine favor (now offered you) and be reconciled to God." (2 Corinthians 5:20 - AMP)

The calling of every born-again believer can be found in Matthew 22:37-40. Here is what Jesus so emphatically laid out: Jesus said to him, "You shall love the Lord your God with all your heart, with all your soul, and with all your mind.

This is the first and great commandment. And the second is like it: You shall love your neighbor as yourself.

On these two commandments hang all the Law and the Prophets."

Let me start by saying that a person cannot give what they don't have! They can't talk about something (with full authority and assurance) that they themselves have not experienced.

Think of a salesman making every effort trying to sell you fishing equipment, but what if he himself had never gone out fishing? What would he suggest for bait on a freshwater pond, or in deep sea fishing? He wouldn't even know what times are best for fishing — either morning or night.

The same thing goes for those who have religion but have never encountered the living Christ! How would you be able to share about forgiveness, mercy, and grace, if you have never experienced them? How would you be able to say that He saves to the utmost degree if He has not yet saved you? Do you see it?

Ambassadors for Christ

In this devotion today, I want to bring forth the heart behind a sale. The Scripture says that God is making His appeal as it were through us. For this to take place, we must enter God's heart, and He must enter ours! There is no other way to experience God but through this powerful and loving exchange.

Once we experience His love and mercy, we will be ready to share that very embedding experience with others. We will not only know it by our own experience of it, but we would have tasted of the Lord's goodness and found out firsthand, that the Lord is good!

How can we talk about the Lord's goodness unless we had tasted of Him ourselves?

Time to Sit Under His Shadow and Learn!

1. Have you ever been a salesperson for any product? Share it with the group.

2. When you became a salesperson, did they train you on the product? What was the product and what did they teach you? Share with the group.

3. Did you know that when you were born-again, you also became an ambassador for Christ? What is your description of an ambassador? Discuss with the group.

4. Knowing the Lord intimately gives you authority and

knowledge of who God is. Once you know who He is to you, you will be able to share Him with others who don't know Him.

5. Make it your aim to be an ambassador for Jesus! Take the good news of the gospel of the kingdom with you everywhere you go (this includes your home, your work, your school, on vacation, etc.). If not you, then who? If not now, then when?

Day 6

Having Nothing and Yet Possessing All Things!

"...as having nothing, and yet possessing all things." (2 Corinthians 6:10)

"And the Lord said to Abram, after Lot had separated from him: 'Lift your eyes now and look from the place where you are—northward, southward, eastward, and westward; for all the land which you see I give to you and your descendants forever. And I will make your descendants as the dust of the earth; so that if a man could number the dust of the earth, then your descendants also could be numbered. Arise, walk in the land through its length and its width, for I give it to you.'" (Genesis 13:14-17)

Let me start by saying that if you have Jesus, whether you know it or not, you have everything!

The world looks at outward things as important and valuable; but the spiritual person looks at life as a gift from God.

If the Lord gave life, then we conclude that He will also keep it going, until He has fulfilled His plan.

Let us look at a few things and meditate upon these mindsets.

For starters, let us look at the life of the Apostle Paul. Once touched by the Lord, Paul was on a rampage to convert the whole world into becoming followers of Jesus. He did not count His life and all its inconveniences as hindrances or obstacles in his endeavor! Paul counted all things as loss for the sake of Christ.

Also, let us focus on the life of Abraham when he allowed his nephew, Lot to choose what piece of land he wanted to take.

Though Abraham was the called one and should have had first choice in the choosing, he allowed his nephew Lot to go first! This is how much value Abraham put on materialism (lands and things) that he allowed his nephew to go first.

When we know the Lord in an intimate way, we will know secrets and have insight that nobody has a clue about. This is an amazing mindset!

I believe that consequently, when we allow material things to take hold of our hearts, they will paralyze our ability to please God. This enslaving mindset of materialism impacts our life of faith like nothing else. When we begin to bow to our lower nature (carnal nature) and pay attention to what we see, what we feel, or what we hear, and not see life from God's perspective, we will end up stalling and even aborting God's plan for our lives all together.

Time to Sit Under His Shadow and Learn!

1. In reading the words, **"...as having nothing, and yet possessing all things."** (2 Corinthians 6:10) What is your interpretation of this? Discuss with your study group.

2. When you hear materialism what comes to mind? Discuss with the group.

3. In Genesis 13:14-17, Abraham taught us all a great lesson(s). What lessons did God teach you in this reading? Share with a group and discuss.

4. Have you ever been hindered by a materialistic mindset? How did it hinder your life? Share with

the group and discuss.

5. Are you willing to lose everything to have more of Jesus in your life? If your answer is a sincere yes, then share with the group how you will be living this out on a daily basis.

Day 7

It's Time to Step It Up!

"He who walks with wise men will be wise..." (Proverbs 13:20)

There are times that we say to ourselves, I need to change! Or I need to do more of this and less of that!

I do believe most of us desire the highest good in life. We truly desire to be the best dad, mom, son, daughter, employee, pastor, servant, etc. We all have this great expectation to some degree.

Now, regarding all these different aspirations, we must change to meet the demand that we want to see. To wish and desire different results without changing ourselves, will only give us more of the same. To think that our lives will be altered by just wishing, is setting ourselves up for some major disappointments.

In the words of King Solomon, he teaches that those who **"walk with wise men will be wise."**

It is interesting to see how the wise are more particular in the way they think, speak and act. When you meet a wise person, you will know that they are wise. They don't have to wear a tee-shirt that says, "I AM WISE!" They don't have to wear a silly cap that says, "I am full of Wisdom!" You just know.

My advice is that when you meet a wise individual, make every effort to get to know them and befriend them. It will bring you to a higher realm in your endeavors.

The Fool

What is amazing to me is that the opposite is also true.

The fool, also, is very particular in the way he thinks, speaks, and acts. He cannot help himself get out of a paper bag! He only finds negativity everywhere he turns; everything is chaotic, everything goes wrong, and it just seems (and maybe it's just me thinking this) but everything he touches, he destroys! Maybe a little exaggeration, but just a little.

Do you know individuals like the one I am describing here? I believe you do.

Now, please understand that I am not criticizing the fool, God knows that we have done our share of foolish things. But doing a foolish thing doesn't constitute you being a fool, but a lifestyle of foolish decisions, will get you the fool's trophy! I am basically saying all this to bring about the contrast between a wise and a foolish person.

Guess what? We get to choose who we want to be — a wise or a foolish person. The real beauty to all this is that we get to choose what kind of future we want to have!

Time to Sit Under His Shadow and Learn!

1. Do you aspire to change things in your life, whether natural or spiritual? If you do, share with your group.

2. What significant changes have you made in the last 6 months? This would be good to do openly with the group and allow God to speak as you share.

3. Can you describe the difference between a wise person and a foolish one? Discuss this in group format.

4. Have you done foolish things that have had severe consequences to you or your family, etc.? Please share with the group.

5. Are you willing to pay the price and become wise for the sake of the kingdom of God? Share with the group.

Day 8

Don't Be a Stupid Fellow!

"But the companion of fools will be destroyed." (Proverbs 13:20)

In meditating on this verse for the past two days, I have really been drilling this specific word into my heart and spirit. The need to be wise or wiser is now— to shun foolishness must be one or our highest priorities today, especially as we see the world turning into chaos!

As I have been pondering what kind of man I want to become, I am also faced with the challenge of the person I don't want to become — the fool.

In my devotion today, I want to bring forth several characteristics of the fool. I pray that we will be able to see through my simple words and embrace the reality of what it truly means to be a fool and hopefully not end up as one!

A Stupid Fellow

When we say stupid to someone, we are literally telling them that they are fools. Now, are they really fools? Perhaps they don't know what they don't know and they speak things that they have no knowledge on. It's a possibility.

Nevertheless, fools are very distinct in nature and character. Let me give you a few noticeable traits in a fool's life:

The fool hates knowledge [Proverbs 1:22]. He doesn't want to know more than what he knows. He usually is content with his own worldview and what he sees and thinks— is what it is! The simple fact that he won't see outside of his own viewpoint is setting him up for committing foolish things repeatedly!

The fool DOES NOT delight in understanding [Proverbs 18:2]. Another interesting thing about a fool, is that though he doesn't know what he ought to know — but he thinks he does! Does this make sense?

The fool does mischief as a sport [Proverbs 10:23]. What is mischief? To incite wickedness and laugh about it. The fool gets his joy out of inciting wickedness. It excites him to see others fail, lose, or come down in disgrace!

The fool proclaims with his heart [Proverbs 12:23], *with his mouth* [Proverbs 15:2] and *feeds on it* [Proverbs 15:14].

Obviously, the fool is consumed with this lifestyle that it oozes out of him, yes, through his heart, his mouth, and he feeds on it to top it off!

Time to Sit Under His Shadow and Learn!

1. As a group, spend some time meditating upon this word. What kind of man or woman do you want to resemble in your life?

2. Have you ever called a person stupid? Did you know what the word stupid meant? Share with the group.

3. On this one devotion, an outline of what a fool looks like, has been laid out. Do you know any fools in your life?

4. As you walk with God, what are some of the things you can do to make sure you don't fall into a fool's

category? Share with a group.

5. The Bible says that the fear of the Lord is the beginning of wisdom. Fearing (reverencing) the Lord is where it all starts. Are you walking in holy reverence toward God? Share with the group.

Day 9

For Your Sakes!

"For you know the grace of our Lord Jesus Christ, that though He was rich, yet for your sakes He became poor, that you through His poverty might become rich." (2 Corinthians 8:9)

Learning to live and be like Jesus Christ our Lord is the greatest challenge for any disciple of His. Jesus is the example of how one should live and act on this earth.

Meditating upon this one verse, the Holy Spirit reminds us of how Christ Himself did things not for His own gain, but rather sought always to please the Father. His goal was first to do all that the Father wanted Him to do, and secondly, to share His life with all of us who had no hope; we who were lost and undone without God!

Giving His Riches Away!

An interesting fact about Christ was that although He was rich and really had need for anything, He still willfully chose to give His life away as a ransom for us who had no hope! This is love!

Christ didn't come to the world to add to its population, He came into the world with an intention to change it! He was sent forth with a burning passion and mission to seek and save those who were lost!

Fully Yielded!

To be able to do what Christ did, one must first yield their good name, their treasures, and their already established lifestyles. It is necessary to give yourself away into the hands of God and allow Him to use you as He wills.

Surrendering all you are and all that you hope to become in the future, is not an easy thing to do! As a matter of fact, few do this! Serving Christ has in its spiritual fiber the need to give away your riches so that others can be rich. It's a lifestyle that becomes more and more about others and their spiritual well-being, than your own plans and ambitions.

The Scripture says something powerful: **"...Christ, that**

though He was rich, yet for your sakes He became poor..."

Do you get this? To be like Jesus entails a life of surrender for the sake of others. Now, I don't believe that one must empty their bank account for this to be possible. I believe the Scripture mentions this life of surrender more as a principle of giving your life away to God (whatever that may entail) for the sake of others — to experience the power of the living Christ in them, through your witness!

As we open our lives to the Lord, ask Him to give you a vision of who Christ really is, and what He is calling you to do on a personal level.

Time to Sit Under His Shadow and Learn!

1. Are you a disciple of the Lord Jesus? If you consider yourself a disciple, what have you found to be the biggest challenges as you follow Him? Share and discuss with your study group.

2. Have you ever been challenged by the Lord to give some thing away (money, time, other resources, etc.)? Share with the group.

3. Are you presently living a life full of passion for Jesus? Has He challenged you to give more of yourself than what you already have? Discuss this point with the group.

4. Everything we do for Jesus, is for the sake of others. How do these words, "for the sake of others" affect you? Discuss with the group.

5. What is the Holy Spirit calling you to do as you follow Christ with all your heart? Share this with the group.

Day 10

The Cross Test!

**"Commit your works to the Lord,
And your thoughts will be established."** (Proverbs 16:3)

As I spent time in prayer today, I came across this portion of Scripture in Proverbs 16:3. An interesting revelation that the Holy Spirit caused me to see today was the word commit. Commit, in its original Hebrew understanding means to roll out.

If we put it in context, the writer of these proverbs is saying that we are to **"...roll our work to the Lord."** Do you see this?

In other words, we are to bring out (roll out) our deepest longings to the Lord. We are to open our hearts with full assurance to the Holy Spirit. He can be trusted with our emotions, our fears, our doubts, and any lack we might have!

Our Plans!

In going back to the will of God, anyone can understand it if they truly desire to know it. It only takes humility and allowing the Holy Spirit to confirm that our plans are in accordance with His. In committing to God our plans, He can now search for our deepest motivations.

Once the Holy Spirit inspects our heart's desires and motivations He will approve or disapprove of our wishes. If God is to allow us to continue with what we desire, then He will bring it to pass. Listen to this word: **"Now this is the confidence that we have in Him, that if we ask anything according to His will, He hears us. And if we know that He hears us, whatever we ask, we know that we have the petitions that we have asked of Him."** (1 John 5:14-15)

The second part to this devotion is that as we roll our work to the Lord, our thoughts will then be established.

Hear the Spirit of the Lord— as we commit (roll) our work to the Lord, our thoughts will be established. There must be alignment between our heart and mind if we are to move in God's favor!

As I close today's devotion, let us learn to take every idea through the cross test. Ask yourself the question, Is this idea about making me sound smart and great, or does it glorify Jesus?

Time to Sit Under His Shadow and Learn!

1. What does committing something to the Lord mean to you? Are there things in your life that you have not committed to the Lord? Discuss and share in your study group.

2. Have you been honest with the Lord about what you truly feel about life in general? Discuss with the group.

3. What was the last thing you opened your heart to God for?? Was it a decision, a person, a situation? Share and discuss with the group.

4. God does know our hearts. What do you think God would find you thinking about if He were to ask you right now?

5. Spiritual alignment basically means that you are aligned with God's agenda. Do you find yourself in the center of God's will today?

Day 11

It Seems Right!

**"There is a way that seems right to a man,
But its end is the way of death."** (Proverbs 16:25)

During my quiet time with God today, I found this one proverb that reminded me so much of a comment my mentor and pastor said to me many years ago. He told me, "David—anybody can convince themselves that they bought a good used car!" Let me explain what my pastor was referring to.

There were some people in the church (actually, a family) who were going through a difficult situation and were seeking counsel. They came to our church and met up with the pastor. As the pastor started to give them counsel regarding the matter at hand, they kept blocking his counsel, and they wouldn't receive anything from him. These individuals kept making excuses for their actions and why it was so unfair what they were presently facing.

My pastor proceeded to tell them that maybe the decisions that they had made were not the best decisions. Though they heard the counsel, they insisted that their way of doing things was correct and so forth. At the end of the meeting, nothing was resolved, and they left thinking that they were right all along, when they were not!

What does this story have to do with Proverbs 16:25? Well, pretty much everything!

You see, there are sometimes solutions that seem right to certain people.. Yes, they seem right, but they are not! As a matter of fact, this is the way to death. In reading this verse and in the words, it seems- what makes an individual miss the mark or take the wrong path? What constitutes a bad action or decision?

Decisions that lead to death are decisions that are made out of God's timing; they are forced and even manipulated to give us a favorable outcome!

One thing I have learned in my walk with the Spirit of God is: If we must push, force, or manipulate something to happen, it is almost certain that it is not God leading us!

Time to Sit Under His Shadow and Learn!

1. In reading Proverbs 16:25, have you ever been stubborn with God? If you have been a stubborn individual, share it with your group.

2. Have you found out the hard way, that when you attempt to force something— it never really works out for you? Share your story with the group.

3. What about your decision making? Do you wait upon the Lord or godly leadership for the green light?

4. I believe we all have made bad decisions at one time or another. What lessons have you learned from some bad decisions you have made in your life? List them and then share them with your group.

5. I have found out that the peace of God must be the emotion that resembles God's green light. Never confirm anything as approved by God until you have His peace!

Day 12

Giving from the Heart!

"But this I say: He who sows sparingly will also reap sparingly, and he who sows bountifully will also reap bountifully. So let each one give as he purposes in his heart, not grudgingly or of necessity; for God loves a cheerful giver." (2 Corinthians 9:6, 7)

Let me first address the law of sowing and reaping. We will never live our lives without this one universal law. This law has been instituted by God in the universe, and it will respond no matter what we do. The results of this law are based on our actions. Whatever we give — we will receive!

In Paul's words, he makes it a point to say that, **"He who sows sparingly, will also reap sparingly, and he who sows bountifully will also reap bountifully."**

In other words, every person who has decided to sow little, will get their just reward, and so the same for the one who sows much— they will reap great rewards.

Now, if we base the results on our sowing, would we not be more mindful of everything we do when it comes to giving?

Now the heart has eyes, and it sees what it wants to give. Do we give based on what we have in our pocket, purse, check book, etc., or do we give what we see inside our heart? Obviously, the choice is totally up to the individual.

Here's another thing to know:

If our giving causes a grudgeful feeling, we will reap that. If our heart gives because it sees a need, this also is not what God is looking for. So, what kind of giving is God looking for? Let's see.

God Loves a Cheerful Giver!

"...for God loves a cheerful giver."

A cheerful giver— what is a cheerful giver? The word cheerful means happy. A cheerful giver is a happy person. It's that simple. They are happy because they know God, they are blessed by God, they have a great future in God, they are happy to be alive, etc.

When an opportunity comes to be an expression of God to others, they happily do it! They are not thinking about what they are getting back, they are not upset because they must give, and as a matter of fact, they are happy to do it!

Let this be us!

Time to Sit Under His Shadow and Learn!

1. Are you aware of the law of sowing and reaping? Do you understand it? Share it with your study group and discuss.

2. Do you practice the laws of sowing and reaping in everything you do? Share your experiences with the group.

3. Have you ever expressed grudgeful feelings when asked to bless someone? Don't be embarrassed to share your experiences with the group.

4. Share with the group the last time you gave with a cheerful heart.

5. If you want to make cheerful giving part of your life, begin to give at every opportunity your heart tells you to.

Day 13

Lending to the Lord!

**"He who has pity on the poor lends to the Lord,
And He will pay back what he has given."** (Proverbs 19:17)

On the same topic as yesterday, I feel the Holy Spirit revisiting my heart and mind with the subject of giving from the heart. For some reason, often the Holy Spirit will keep reminding us of a certain truth that He wants us to put to practice.

On dealing with the poor, we all have them around our lives. All you have to do is take a drive and you will see them under a bridge, at a street corner, in some abandoned alley, or sitting in front of a restaurant waiting for alms from someone. I'm sure you have seen plenty of this.

So what is our position in helping the needy and poor?

Our position as servants of the Lord is first to help them

someway somehow. Ignoring them will not take away our need to extend our love beyond our circle of friends. If they (the poor and needy) are before us, it is because God brought them to us, since we would not dare go to them!

Let's look at the word of God in Proverbs 19:17.

By showing pity to the poor, we are literally lending to the Lord. Can you fathom this? This is a call to a higher level in God.

To lend to the Lord has to be one of the greatest opportunities for us as God's people, to show gratitude to God's creation.

Showing Favor!

Now, showing pity is a very powerful word here in this verse. It means to show favor. Poor people usually don't have anyone to show favor to them. They are battered by negativity and bound by a demonic mindset. We are called to show favor and bring the good news to them. Do you see this? Do you remember when the Lord showed favor to you? I'm sure you do! It is time for us to do it for someone else.

In closing, the Scripture says that God will repay all those who lend to Him. The words pay back mean to be complete. In other words, by giving to the Lord, you will not lack anything— for the Lord Himself will give you back in completeness all you have given Him and then some.

Time to Sit Under His Shadow and Learn!

1. Do you personally know any poor people? Share with your study group.

2. Have you ever made any attempt to help them in some way? If you have, please share with the group, and discuss the blessing behind helping them.

3. Have you ever felt bad for not helping someone when it was in your power to do so? Share this with the group.

4. Lending to the Lord is an opportunity to show the light of Jesus to the lost. Remember how powerful of an impact this will make for His glory!

5. Have you experienced the recompense of the Lord for reaching out and helping the poor? Share this with the group.

Day 14

We Are God's Habitation!

"The spirit of a man is the lamp of the Lord, searching all the inner depths of his heart." (Proverbs 20:27)

How does God keep Himself always engaged with us? I believe God does it through the spirit He gave us when He breathed life into us and made us living beings.

You see, God gave us of His Spirit when we were created—yes, as we were being conceived in our mother's womb. This is an amazing thought!

God's spirit gives us life and remains within us, (though dormant) giving us a conscience that allows us to govern our lives the best way we can. It is not until the day that we receive the knowledge of who God is, that we receive Him into our hearts as Lord and Savior. We call this being born-again of the Spirit.

The Holy Spirit will come down from heaven and take man's

heart as His home. We then become a habitation for God in the Spirit. We become God's house!

This was and will always be God's desire!

The Lord longs to live within us and lead and guide our lives into His desired end. It is not about where I want to go or what I want to be; it is all about why He created us and what His intentions are for us.

None of us know the way without the Holy Spirit showing us where to go and what to do. It is the Spirit that carries our very own personal blueprint...

"But as it is written:
'Eye has not seen, nor ear heard,
Nor have entered into the heart of man
The things which God has prepared for those who love Him.'
But God has revealed them to us through His Spirit.
For the Spirit searches all things, yes, the deep things of God." (1 Corinthians 2:9-10)

Through God's Spirit, God searches our hearts and can intercede for us. It is through His awesome Spirit, that we are shown all the mysteries, expectations, purpose, and plans of the Lord.

Time to Sit Under His Shadow and Learn!

1. Have you opened your heart to the Holy Spirit and invited Him in to come and make His home in you? Share this question with your study group. If someone has not done this, ask them if they would like to make their hearts a place for God to dwell? Lead them in the sinner's prayer and have them repeat after you to receive Christ.

   A Sinner's Prayer:
   Lord Jesus, today I come before you as a sinner. I am lost and I need your Holy Spirit to show me the way. I confess that I am a person who has committed many sins against You. Please forgive me for all my sins. Cleanse me with Your precious blood that was shed at the cross for me. I now receive Your gift of salvation. Please come and live in my heart and never let me go! I want to serve You with my whole heart from this day on! Amen.

2. When the Spirit of the Lord comes to live within us,

He will show us what to do, how to do it, and where to go. Ask yourself the question: Am I allowing the Holy Spirit to lead my life? Discuss this with the group.

3. Have you ever lived your life outside of what God's Spirit wanted out of you? Discuss this point with the group.

4. Can you tell the difference now that the Spirit of God is leading you versus the way you used to live before He came into your heart? Share some of the different ways God has been leading you with the group.

5. What has been the latest thing the Spirit of God has talked to you about? Share this experience with the group.

Day 15

Discerning the Works of Darkness!

"For Satan himself transforms himself into an angel of light." (2 Corinthians 11:14)

It is interesting that the Apostle Paul puts an emphasis on how the demonic forces transform themselves into something positive, something good. Too many times, believers can't tell that Satan is really the one, behind some selfish scheme. We must always remember that we who walk with God, live on a battlefield. To ignore this — is to set ourselves for some big trouble!

Let me shed some light on 2 Corinthians 11:14, and more specifically, on the word transform. Paul said that **"Satan himself transforms himself."**

It sounds comical, but it is true. Satan puts on a different jump-suit or costume depending on the occasion. He will do this to blend in with just about anyone.

Most people are not very good at discerning the devil's tactics or schemes. As a matter of fact, some people think the devil is really a good helpful friend. People may show up at your front door selling you a perfect plan, yet dipped in selfishness and greed, and you may never even see it.

The Devil Knows

When the devil moves in, it is usually not without an agenda. The devil knows when your guard has been let down, and that we are just a magnet for what he has to offer. He will come in subtly at first, and then will make a stronger move until he reaches his goal.

There is something to be said about a life filled with the Spirit of God — it won't let sin entice, seduce, or position itself in the servant of the Lord. A spirit-filled life is the life of Christ!

Here's what the devil knows: He knows when God's presence is not strong in us. He can tell by the things we do in secret. He knows that we are no longer praying and reading God's word like we need to; He can tell that our desires are not set on things above but rather of things of earth. Oh, he knows!

Full of God's Presence

When we are full of God's presence, we can discern anything that the enemy has prepared. We will be able to see for miles and miles. Is it any wonder why the devil makes every attempt to keep us away from developing a life of prayer, a life of devotion unto Christ?

One of the key things we get when we spend time with God is our discernment. Our discernment is sharpened and the power to overcome is overhauled. Obviously, ignoring our spiritual life will give us the direct opposite.

It is time to seek the Lord and let His glory shine forth. The Scripture says that His enemies melt like wax at the presence of the Lord!

Time to Sit Under His Shadow and Learn!

1. Have you seen the devil dress up into an angel of light? Share with your study group.

2. Can you tell the difference between an honest godly per son and an angel of light?

3. What differentiates these two people? List some of the characteristics along with the group.

4. The presence of God sends the devil running. Are you making sure that you are full of His presence? Share with your study group.

5. Discernment is a weapon from the Lord and personal prayer sharpens it! How is your discernment these days? Share with the group and discuss.

Day 16

Disciplined Lifestyle!

"He who loves pleasure will be a poor man; He who loves wine and oil will not be rich." (Proverbs 21:17)

As I pondered this verse repeatedly, I realized how easy it is to falter into the lesser things of life and abandon what is valuable. It is not hard to let go of the practices that guarantee success!

How often have we all begun something with such intensity and with great emotion, only to see it collapse because of our lack of discipline to keep it going? This is all too common. Anyone can talk a big game, but when it comes down to walking it out, when the time to show some tangible fruit arrives — I'm afraid that there might not be anything there to demonstrate!

The disciplined lifestyle is the hardest way to live, but the most rewarding. Many don't know the secret to a good life.

They can't see beyond their obstacles and their unfortunate situations.

As a matter of fact, I believe the people with the most trouble are those who are undisciplined. May the Lord help us to develop discipline in every area of our life. Here are some areas.

The mind. We must learn to discipline our thoughts. Our thoughts govern our actions. Whatever our thoughts see — is what we will pursue! It is that very thing that will dominate our attitude and eventually our actions. Now, if the Lord Jesus is high priority in our minds, we will tend to Him. It is not what we say about Him, but what we do with Him, that establishes us.

One more thing, our time. Time is pretty much irreversible. If we don't take care of our time, someone else will. God is limitless when it comes to time, but we are not! We have 24 hours in a day. To the degree that we make time work for us, is to the degree that we will be on top of our game. If we spend our time on worthless things, then we will reap worthlessness.

I shared just a few elements that we must discipline ourselves in. We can begin here and in time look for other areas that will help us advance.

Time to Sit Under His Shadow and Learn!

1. When you think of the word discipline, what comes to mind? Share with the study group and discuss this.

2. Have you ever started something, but didn't finish? How many times have you done this in 12 months? Share with the group.

3. Would you consider yourself a person who carries out a disciplined lifestyle? If you are, share with the study group what are some of the areas that you have conquered.

4. It would also be good to share some of your struggles in some of the areas of your life where you need to establish discipline.

5. The mind and time are two major things to discipline. Make every effort to bring these two areas under subjection and make them work for you not against you!

Day 17

Excuses, Excuses, Excuses!

**"The lazy man says, 'There is a lion outside!
I shall be slain in the streets!'"** (Proverbs 22:13)

When one is young and inexperienced in life, one tends to make so many mistakes— mistakes that are outright foolish. Why do we make them? Because we are inexperienced, extremely proud, and quite foolish!

When asked why we made a certain decision that brought a lot of pain, we just shrug our shoulders and say, I don't really know! We all have made these gestures and to some degree, (even as we have gotten older in age) we will continue to make them.

Someone once said, "The older we get, the wiser we become."

That may be true in some respect, but not completely. I have seen some older people make some terrible and awful mistakes. Sometimes, the mistakes compound into one tragic mistake after another. Does this sound familiar to you?

When confronted with a predicament, people will make excuses when things do not go as expected. Yes, as we get older, we become smarter (but sometimes, too much for our own good)!

Ownership Needed.

Nothing produces change in us like a good reality check. We need to take ownership for our lives, mistakes included. To pass the buck or shift the blame to someone else only hurts us. Unless we take ownership of all the good and all the bad that happens to us, we will never outgrow our need to make excuses!

Truth be told —the more excuses we make, the less credibility we have. The more we practice irresponsibility, the more we negate opportunities in our life. The more excuses we invent, the less valuable we become as people.

Apologize Sincerely - But Why?

When failing to show up to something, when you promised to be present, one must make restitution. I believe one must make the necessary connection with the one who originally invited you to the event and apologize sincerely for not showing up! This will in turn, keep the communication lines open, and provide a bridge for being invited the next time there is an event.

Don't just disappear and think that it is ok to not show up to a promised event. It is not only rude but also extremely irresponsible! Remember, what you sow is what you reap!

Time to Sit Under His Shadow and Learn!

1. What would you consider a foolish mistake in your own life? List some examples and share with your study group.

2. Have you ever felt trapped by your own mistakes and had to lie to hide another previous lie— all for the sake of not embarrassing yourself? Share with the group this one point.

3. What does taking ownership mean to you? Define this and share with the group. I believe this is one

major area that needs to be addressed among young people in today's world. Emphasize this point.

4. Can you define what it means to apologize sincerely? Discuss this among your group.

5. Learn to build good relationships with people. Relationships are like flowers in a garden. Cultivate them with love and with patience. Discuss this with your group.

Day 18

Don't Set Your Eyes on What Is Not!

"Do not overwork to be rich;
Because of your own understanding, cease!
Will you set your eyes on that which is not?
For riches certainly make themselves wings;
They fly away like an eagle toward heaven." (Proverbs 23:4, 5)

"For where your treasure is, there your heart will be also." (Matthew 6:21)

It takes great humility to go past the preferable. What is preferable?? The preferable thing is that thing that you want and must have no matter who or what gets in the way. Do you have things that are preferable?

Now, let me take you a step deeper in this devotion.

Usually, things that are preferable are things that, for the most part, are accommodating to the flesh and are usually not God's will for us. These things are things that the Lord told us repeatedly not to indulge in! Does it make sense now?

In the verses above, I felt the Holy Spirit leading me to share on things that are of eternal value. Let's spend some time on this one proverb...

"Do not overwork to be rich;"
These words can be argued, and we can probably debate the principle, if its source was someone who had a misunderstanding of what being rich was all about. The problem here is that it was Solomon who made the statement. King Solomon was the richest king in the whole known world. Why would he be saying, Do not overwork to be rich? Hmm.... He adds to his powerful point the following and says, "Because of your understanding, cease!"
Wow.

In other words, King Solomon in essence is saying, You know better than this. Why are you beating yourself up to make a little money? Stop it already!

After bringing about this evaluation to the forefront, he says,

"Will you set your eyes on what is not?"

This has to be one of the most profound interrogational questions to the human soul and calls out those who pursue vain things saying, Will you set your eyes on what is not?

We must learn to swim deep in the river of God's presence, so that the "things that are not," will be exposed, severed, and our freedom restored to pursue the things that please Him!

Time to Sit Under His Shadow and Learn!

1. Have you ever been challenged by God's Spirit to let go of something or to embrace something pertaining to His will? How was your challenge? Share with your study group.

2. Humility means God must be first in all things. Are you walking in humility?

3. We must learn to discern what is of the Lord and what is not. How is your discernment these days? Share with the group.

4. "Will you set your eyes on things that are not?" What do these words mean to you? Share this with the group and discuss.

5. Whatever does not produce or bring peace in your heart, know that this lack of peace does not come from the Lord. Know where you are standing with God at all times. Discuss this with your study group.

Day 19

Exalted Above Measure?

"And lest I should be exalted above measure by the abundance of the revelations, a thorn in the flesh was given to me, a messenger of Satan to buffet me, lest I be exalted above measure." (2 Corinthians 12:7)

Having read this portion of Scripture countless times, I am always refreshed when I read God's word with the heart to understand God's true or original intention.

One of man's greatest stumbling blocks is an arrogant heart and a life full of pride. Pride and arrogance go hand in hand, yes, and they both work for a common purpose— to separate us from the grace and favor of God! Here's what James 4:6 says in his letter regarding the matter:

"But He gives more grace. Therefore He says:
'God resists the proud,
But gives grace to the humble.'"

In another place the Scripture reads:

"Therefore, humble yourselves under the mighty hand of God, that He may exalt you in due time." (1 Peter 5:6)

To all this, God has made provision. He has arranged our lives in such a way that we are kept in check. First, by the Holy Spirit's prompting, and secondly, by living under His mighty hand and experiencing certain situations (the tests and trials) in life. Are you understanding God's ways now?

In the case of the Apostle Paul, God had shown him incredible or unbelievable insight into the realm of the Spirit. He was taken up to paradise, to the third heaven. He was a recipient of God's glorious revelations and received wisdom and teaching from the Lord Himself.

What a privilege to be handpicked by God for this powerful experience!

Along with the glorious revelations, God also did something that seemed puzzling at first; He gave the Apostle Paul a thorn in the flesh, and the enemy of Satan to buffet him.

Now why would God allow this? Did the enemy force himself on Paul and attack him just because Paul had seen God? Of course not! God was not concerned about the devil one bit; He was concerned about Paul and his human side!

God had to do something that would get the Apostle Paul dependent upon God every day from that moment forward.

You and I will experience brokenness somehow. If you want to be a man or woman of God, the Lord Himself will bring you and I to such a place!

Time to Sit Under His Shadow and Learn!

1. Have you ever recognized arrogance and pride in yourself? If you have, please share with your study group.

2. How did the Lord personally teach you to overcome pride and arrogance? Or has it been a continuous struggle for you? Share with the group.

3. You must know that the devil always leverages on our weaknesses. He can't force us to sin, but He can use our weakness to his advantage. Share with the group this point and discuss.

4. If we don't humble ourselves willingly, He will humble us forcefully! All of this is because He loves us. Share this thought and exchange comments with the group.

5. We must never try to go past the measure of the sphere that God has given us. God will do His best to keep us in line, but if we persist and get our way, it will end up painfully! What do you think of this? Share your comments with the group.

Day 20

You Have to Know Your Place!

"...For in nothing was I behind the most eminent apostles, though I am nothing." (2 Corinthians 12:11)

"But God has chosen the foolish things of the world to put to shame the wise..." (1 Corinthians 1:27)

"He must increase, but I must decrease." (John 3:30)

Acknowledging to ourselves and to others that we are nothing, is truly a great accomplishment. Too many often have the idea that they are something special and that they should be catered to. In the kingdom of God, the servant of the Lord is God's servant! He is the King and has the preeminence in everything!

As I started meditating upon the Apostle Paul's words, I quickly realized that Paul was not out to make a name for himself. He was God's servant, and he knew his place. Too many people don't know their place!

In another Scripture Paul alludes to this and says, **"I am what I am by the grace of God."**

Acknowledging that God is everything and that we are nothing must be a key component in the message we preach.

It is amazing how God can choose weak, foolish, and pretty messed up people to do His bidding. He always chose those who couldn't help themselves. It is God's method— He takes what is lowly and converts them into a mighty force for His name's sake. To God alone be the glory!

Now, for anyone who wants to go deeper into the heart of God, listen to John the Baptist's story.

Here's a man who was sent by God to be a prophetic voice to those who would be passing by on their way to another town along the Jordan River. Though He was chosen by God and for God purposes only — John the Baptist still knew his place in God.

Once John was asked if he was the messiah. He responded, **"I am not!"**

He could have said he was a man sent from God; He could have used his calling as a credential to appear more spiritual than his contemporaries, but He did not! Instead, John said, **"He must increase, but I must decrease."**

My friends, we must know our place.

Time to Sit Under His Shadow and Learn!

1. What do the words **"I am nothing"** mean to you? Share this with your study group as an opening question.

2. Have you ever felt like you were "something," like something special that everyone should be catering to? Discuss your insights with the group.

3. God chose the **"foolish things of the world to confound the wise."** What does this set of words bring into your mind? Let your group give you their own understanding of this and discuss it.

4. Would you consider yourself someone who God chose although you might not deserve it? Discuss with the group.

5. Are you seeking to be recognized by your peers, or is your desire really to exalt King Jesus by your actions? Bounce this idea around with your study group.

Day 21

Build It Twice!

**"Prepare your outside work,
Make it fit for yourself in the field;
And afterward build your house."** (Proverbs 24:27)

I really like what I just read here in Proverbs 24:27 regarding the building of a house. Let me show you what the Holy Spirit said to me about this:

First, we should always build with the end in mind. Never start a project of any kind until you have seen what it will look like when it is finished. Think it, draw it, design it on paper first, then purchase your material and start constructing.

In the wisdom of God, one must prepare the outside work first. What does this mean? It means that we must settle everything in our minds first. Then, we tally the cost and determine if it will be possible to build what we desire.

The first step is to look at the field and see where exactly the house will be built. Will it be constructed on one side, in the center of the field, towards the back or front, or will it take the whole lot to fit it?

The second step will be to build your foundation. The foundation is probably one of the most important steps in building a house. It must be done correctly. Now, if it is laid carelessly, it may crack, break, or be uneven, all affecting the future of that house.

In building anything, don't wing it. There is the correct method to building something that will be strong, solid, and beautiful. The downside, if there is one, is that one must be extremely patient to do it right. You can't hurry to do good work! Don't be irresponsible with the proper steps of building.

Once the work has been done outside, or it has been settled in our hearts and minds, we are ready to do the fun part—the actual house. You see, everything starts in the spirit and then it is manifested in the natural. The hardest part of building anything is its foundation. Once the foundation is laid, the actual house can now be seen.

Time to Sit Under His Shadow and Learn!

1. Have you ever heard the words, begin with the end in mind? What do these words say to you on a personal level? Discuss with your group and share your own understanding of it.

2. Have you ever started a project and failed to prepare its foundation? What was the outcome? Did you see a colossal failure? Share your story with the group.

3. What about the time when you built something and did the necessary preparations? How did this turn out for you? Share with the group.

4. Have you ever had a vision from the Lord to do something special for Him, but you failed to prepare for it, and ended up aborting the whole idea? Share this experience with your group and discuss.

5. In the Lord, everything is birthed in the spirit first, and then it is up to you and I to manifest it! Share your thoughts on this.

Day 22

What Is Tying You Down?

**"Take away the dross from silver,
And it will go to the silversmith for jewelry."** (Proverbs 25:4)

In my meditation this morning, as I pondered one more time the infallible Word of God, I came across this one passage. I thought to myself about how God always knows all things including the deep things that no one knows. As a matter of fact, He knows our own hearts better than we know ourselves!

As I prayed over this one verse, it was here where the Holy Spirit caused me to see how some things can hinder us from reaching our full potential.

In the wisdom of God, He sees our deficiencies, our shortcomings, our sins, our faults and knows that we are imperfect and incomplete. Through the Holy Spirit He will make sure to purify us and bring us to the place where we need to be with Him.

What is Hindering Us?

Have you ever wondered why your life is the way it is? Have you considered all the hindrances that hold you back from your God-given vision?

In your estimation, you have felt that you should be at a much higher level but are barely getting by. Why do you think this is? Do you need to be purified from things that cling to your life and bring and slow you down?

You might feel like you are making some headway only to take steps back when you are about to have a breakthrough. There is a reason for this!

The Race!

"Therefore, we also, since we are surrounded by so great a cloud of witnesses, let us lay aside every weight, and the sin which so easily ensnares us, and let us run with endurance the race that is set before us, looking unto Jesus, the author and finisher of our faith..." (Hebrews 12:1, 2)

In the race of faith, we must lay aside every weight and sin that so easily ensnares us. We can't afford to let anything hinder us:, especially anything personal and certainly nothing from others!

It's until we put off what hinders us that we will advance in our own race for His glory.

Time to Sit Under His Shadow and Learn!

1. Have you experienced specific hindrances in your own life; things that have held you back from reaching a certain goal, etc.? If you have, take time to share with your group.

2. How did you recognize these hindrances? Share with the group.

3. Did it take you some time to recognize your hindrance? Did someone else point it out to you, did the Holy Spirit reveal it to you?

4. Did you have a hard time admitting that you were being hindered by such things? If you struggled admitting anything, share that thought process with

the group.

5. Sin is heavy to carry, and you will quickly tire trying to hold onto it. The best thing to do when you know you have a hindrance of sin holding you back is to confess and forsake that sin—Then you will soar!

Day 23

On Becoming Complete

"Finally, brethren, farewell. Become complete. Be of good comfort, be of one mind, live in peace; and the God of love and peace will be with you." (2 Corinthians 13:11)

What exactly are you pursuing in God? What is it that keeps you searching or seeking in life? What makes you stay up at nights? What is that thing that keeps you dreaming for so much more? What does your mind dwell upon?

As a believer and follower of Jesus, you have ambitions, holy ambitions. There is a reason for these emotions moving within us.. What exactly does God want you and I to reach?

My Passion . . .

Let me just say that in my years of seeking God, I have found that what I am truly longing for is an ongoing encounter with the living God and the life transformation that will make an impact in my world and in my generation.

Becoming complete for me is nothing more and nothing less than becoming all that Jesus designed me to be!

What Does It Mean?

Let's look at the word complete in its original language.

The word complete means to be made or become ready, suitable, or equipped in advance for a particular purpose or for some use or event. It also means to adjust, put in order, or restore.

Though we might think that our way of being is what God has designed— we are usually wrong. God has so much more for us!

Full of Ourselves!

In our minds we tend to think that we are just right the way we are. Yet, once we begin to look at the face of God, we quickly realize that God's idea is very different from the one we hold. His presence begins to show us how different we are than what He has intended for us.

To be complete simply means that we get the mind of God and think like God, move like God, and do the works of God!

Let us aspire to be complete in Him. This is the high calling of God in Christ Jesus.

Time to Sit Under His Shadow and Learn!

1. Have you ever questioned yourself on what exactly you are pursuing in your Christian experience? Share with your study group.

2. God designed you to be what? Have you discovered this? Share and discuss this with your group.

3. Nothing hinders our flow of God more than when we think we don't need to learn anything new. When someone thinks that they have arrived, it's the beginning of a spiritual collapse. Share this thought and discuss.

4. On a scale of 1 to 10, (1 being lowest and 10 being highest) where would you rank yourself as being complete? Bounce this idea around with your study

group.

5. God has His own mind. He wants to give you His mind so we can be complete in Him. Humble yourself today and allow His Spirit to teach your heart and mind.

Day 24

Communion of the Holy Spirit!

"The grace of the Lord Jesus Christ, and the love of God, and the communion of the Holy Spirit be with you all. Amen." (2 Corinthians 13:14)

As I read this closing line in 2 Corinthians 13:14, I pondered the thought that we must make the Holy Spirit our best friend! How many of us have made the Holy Spirit our dearest and best friend? Truly something to think about and consider.

Our Attitude!

Our attitude toward the Holy Spirit will truly be transformational in us, if we allow Him his rightful place in our hearts.

I have heard believers talk about the Word of God and how we must study it to show ourselves approved as ministers, or how we should pray and spend time with God alone in secret and, how often we should fast and for how long, etc.

To all this I say, yes and amen, but also, There is so much more!

The Person of the Holy Spirit

In our theology, we must know that the Holy Spirit is the One that now lives in us. It is God's Spirit that now dwells richly in us! It is through Him that we know God. Not only does He bring us into Christ's presence, He also lets us know what God is thinking. He will show us the pattern of the Lord and challenge us to walk it out!

Having a great friendship with God the Holy Spirit (the third person of the trinity) is a must if we are to be apostolic and move with God in the world we live in.

Communion

Now in this specific verse, the Apostle Paul brings forth a definite word, He uses the word communion. He says, "**... and the communion of the Holy Spirit be with you all...**"

What is communion of the Holy Spirit? The word communion means participation. In other words, the Lord desires that we make the Holy Spirit a participant of all that we are to do as believers. We do this by allowing Him to take His rightful place in us. He will then lead us accordingly as God wishes.

We can't have a successful life in God without the communion of the Holy Spirit. We must allow ourselves to be led by Him.

Time to Sit Under His Shadow and Learn!

1. What is your belief in the Holy Spirit (the third person of the holy trinity)? Discuss this in your group.

2. Is your life governed by the Holy Spirit? Share and discuss with the group.

3. Have you turned your whole life over to be led by God's Holy Spirit? Share these thoughts with the group.

4. Did you know that the Holy Spirit is the mind of God? Whatever it is that God is thinking, He will reveal it to you through His Spirit. Discuss this with your group.

5. Communion with the Holy Spirit is the highest order of intimacy. Learn to walk in the shadow of His Spirit and you will never lack any good thing. Discuss this point and share your own experience.

Day 25

Are You Responsible for the Assignment?

"Paul, an apostle (not from men nor through man, but through Jesus Christ and God the Father who raised Him from the dead)..."(Galatians 1:1)

Meditating upon Galatians 1:1, my attention is drawn to the call of God that Paul was given- he was to be an apostle for Jesus the King! In this one verse, He specifically says regarding his call, that it was given or revealed, "not from men nor through man."

There is no person in the world who knows what God has intended for us. Only Christ the Lord has this answer. Man can put titles on people, but they are only that, titles! Man can recognize a certain type of gifting upon our lives, and that is all well and good, and we appreciate the gift of recognition.

However, it is God who designed us before we were even born. He called us before we came into our mother's womb. Before anyone could see our face, the Lord already saw it and commissioned us with His assignment.

As Paul reveals that his call was not given by man, he proceeds to show us that his call came from Jesus Christ!

It is Jesus who calls us into our assignment in life. He is the one who makes all these things happen. As far as the specifics of our assignments or calling, the timing of it and the method He will use to reveal this, it is all on Him. He will make these things known to us in His timing.

As we get caught up in worship and taken into His very presence, the Lord will unveil some of these eternal secrets to those who care to find out what they are. Now, not everyone cares to find out what these secrets are; they really don't want to know what God has for them.

Responsibility at the Highest Level

When God calls us to serve Him in some capacity, along with the calling, there is a responsibility attached to it. What is the responsibility? The responsibility is to get as much of it done!

People tend to look around and see what others are doing. Some people find time to compare themselves with others or worse yet, criticize the work of someone else's hands. What a waste of emotions and time this can be!

Remember: We will give accounts of all that we have done and not done with our tasks. With this in future view, we must be about the Father's business; we must tackle the task at hand and know that we will be held accountable for it.

Time to Sit Under His Shadow and Learn!

1. **Have you ever given any thought to the calling or assignment God has given you? Share these thoughts with the group.**

2. **Has God ever revealed to you the assignment for your life? Share this with the group.**

3. **Has anyone ever prophesied over your life and activated God's calling upon your life? Share these thoughts with the group.**

4. Do you feel that you are flowing in God's assignment today? If yes, what does that assignment look like? Share this with the group.

5. With every assignment, God requires responsibility. Are you being responsible with your assignment? Define the word responsibility. Bounce the idea around with your group.

Day 26

Man-Pleasers!

"For if I still pleased men, I would not be a bondservant of Christ." (Galatians 1:10)

What is a man-pleaser? What type of person is this? A man pleaser is somebody who is looking for man's favor, approval, and acceptance. Man-pleasers are those people who work hard on their reputation and hopefully their good works go noticed by others (especially their friends and other contemporaries).

Many believers are still caught up in pleasing man instead of God. They would rather be in good standing with man, rather than have God's approval. My mentor and pastor used to always say, "If I displease God, it doesn't matter who I please. If I please God, then it doesn't matter who I displease!"

I could have not said it better myself.

They Called Themselves Pharisees!

During the times of Jesus, a religious group Jesus called the Pharisees were man-pleasers. They seemed to be more concerned about external works and being seen by others — receiving praise and recognition for their good works. This has always been a temptation for all believers; to think that we need man's approval and acceptance so that we may move forward. This is not true and don't you buy it!

Listen to what Jesus said concerning the Pharisees:

"Woe to you, scribes and Pharisees, hypocrites! For you are like whitewashed tombs which indeed appear beautiful outwardly, but inside are full of dead men's bones and all uncleanness. Even so you also outwardly appear righteous to men, but inside you are full of hypocrisy and lawlessness." (Matthew 23:27, 28)

Pharisees were hypocrites, according to Jesus! These self-righteous people were enamored by people's approval and acceptance. They always did their religious rites and ceremonies in front of people so people would praise them for their good works and lengthy prayers. It made Jesus vomit!

Discern and Distinguish!

Paul said, **"If I still pleased man, I would not be a bondservant of Christ."**

It's either one or the other!

We must discern and distinguish who we are pleasing. As we serve man, we do it as if we were serving Christ. We must always be mindful that whatever we do, we do it unto the Lord, not for recognition, acceptance, or approval!

Time to Sit Under His Shadow and Learn!

1. Do you understand what a man-pleaser is? Please define and share with your study group.

2. Have you found yourself to be one of these man-pleasers? If you have had this experience, would you be so kind and explain to the group. List the things you learned from this experience.

3. Do you know what a Pharisee is? Have you seen these Pharisees throughout the gospels of Christ? Find

some of the Scriptures where Pharisees are called out by Jesus and list what are some of the hypocrisies that they practiced during that time? Share with the group.

4. Define the word hypocrite. What does it mean to you? Have you ever been one? If you have, share what you learned from your experience.

5. We must learn to live for Christ and please Him! What do you and your group think of this one thought? Discuss and share with your study group.

Day 27

On Being Patient . . .

**"Whoever keeps the fig tree will eat its fruit;
So, he who waits on his master will be honored."** (Proverbs 27:18)

I don't think there is anything more mind-boggling than a farmer who sows seeds on his field on Monday only to pack his bags, and leave town for good on Friday of that same week! Where is he going and what about the field that just received seed?

Too many times we have left projects unfinished; projects were left undone simply because we got tired, bored, or didn't see any results coming. It takes a different kind of person to wait patiently for results.

In pondering these thoughts while I meditated upon Proverbs 27:18, I realized that waiting is not the easiest thing for most people. As a matter of fact, patience for anything in life is not only a characteristic of maturity, but also an element needed throughout our lives!

Now in this Scripture, we find some basic wisdom: **"Whoever keeps the fig tree will eat its fruit."**

If we take care of anything and tend to it, it will reward us. In everything we do there is a profit.

Why is it that so many people give up so easily? Why is it that people can't see a project all the way through? The real issue here is that people have adapted more and more to a society that is going fast nowhere!

We presently live in a society that promotes big rewards with little effort. Easy this and easy that. You can have what you want at the push of a button...wow! Isn't that amazing? I have seen people get so upset when they can't find the tv remote— why all the fighting? The fighting is because no one wants to get up and manually change the channels.
We have definitely entered a pampered age!

The second part to this verse says, **"So he who waits on His master will be honored."**

Waiting is truly the key to most of our character deficiencies. If we learn to be patient and learn to wait, we will be honored. The Bible clearly promotes and teaches this.

Time to Sit Under His Shadow and Learn!

1. Have you ever found yourself in desperation because something didn't happen fast enough? Share this and bring it to a discussion with others.

2. Have you seen your attitude change when things didn't go your way? Share and discuss with the group.

3. Have you offended others simply because you were having a bad day? Share with the group.

4. Why were you having a bad day? Was it because things didn't go your way, or someone stole something (time, money, something personal, etc.) from you? Share some insight with your group.

5. If we learn to cultivate all that God gives us - it will yield great rewards for us.

Day 28

The Beauty of Arabia!

"But when it pleased God, who separated me from my mother's womb and called me through His grace, to reveal His Son in me, that I might preach Him among the Gentiles, I did not immediately confer with flesh and blood, nor did I go up to Jerusalem to those who were apostles before me; but I went to Arabia, and returned again to Damascus." (Galatians 1:15-17)

Here's an interesting truth about walking with Jesus:

When Saul of Tarsus (now the Apostle Paul) met Christ face to face on the Damascus Road, His encounter was so powerful and so real that it changed him. You can read this full encounter in the Book of Acts chapter 9.

What is interesting about Saul's encounter (which by the way, was amazing,) is what Saul did afterwards. If you remember the story, he was blinded by the light that shone from heaven and then remained blind for about 3 days. It was Ananias that opened his eyes by laying hands on him and praying for Saul to be filled with the Spirit of God.

Shortly after this, Saul didn't go back to all the former apostles to confer with them about his conversion to Christianity, oh no, he headed to the desert of Arabia. To Arabia, you might ask? Yes, to the desert to be alone with God.

Many scholars believe that in Arabia is where God revealed by His Spirit, the 13 epistles to the body of Christ. Arabia became his feeding ground for divine revelation.

Is it any wonder why the Apostle Paul was so powerful and mighty in speaking and in dealing with the religious groups of his day? This man had not only seen Christ face to face on the Damascus Road but had now heard Christ speak to him face to face in the Arabian desert.

Saul certainly became a man of God by divine revelation and was moved with such certainty.

As we pursue the heart of God in our own lives, we must attend ourselves to the pattern that was set before us in the great Apostle Paul. We must aspire to be a people of revelational knowledge and not just information. This is what makes all the difference in our experience with God. We have grown accustomed to plain teaching without the anointing. We are used to hearing sermons that don't say much. The regular diet for most Christians consists of nothing more than a quick sermon on Sundays and maybe a half-hearted short message on Wednesday and possibly a focusless prayer meeting on another day of the week.

Let me tell you my friend, there must be more than just the norm. We must find our own Arabian experience in the desert of brokenness and frantic seeking after God's own heart. Until we become a people of revelation, we will only remain a people of information.

Time to Sit Under His Shadow and Learn!

1. Have you met Christ face to face or have had a supernatural experience in God? Share with your study group.

2. Does your heart long for more of His presence? Share your heart with the group.

3. Revelation and information are two separate things. Do you know the difference? Please share with the

group and discuss the difference.

4. If you have had a revelation from the Lord, share it with the group. Was there ever a point where the Holy Spirit came to personally walk you through something? Share this.

5. Don't ever be content with what you have — know that there is always more in the river of God! Share the thought and pray it back with the group.

Day 29

Until I Am Satisfied!

**"There are three things that are never satisfied,
Four never say, 'Enough!':
The grave,
The barren womb,
The earth that is not satisfied with water—
And the fire never says, 'Enough!'"** (Proverbs 30:15, 16)

This morning here in His presence, I have been meditating over this one proverb, and my spirit is leaping within me with joy over it. All I can say is that God is awesome in all His ways!

If I could add anything to this one verse it would probably go something like this: and five, a thirst and hunger for a deeper walk with God!

I love this verse. I guess my heart can see the depth of it and longs to press deeper into the heart of the Lord. Something within me says that there is more of Him for me! I can't stop seeking, searching, yearning, and longing for more of His presence in my life. I feel brand new this morning in His awesome presence!

In pursuing hard after thee (the Lord) as the Psalmist said, one must realize that these desires are not taught by any man. This is like deep calling into the deep! This comes from the throne room of God directly into our spirit-man that is inside us.

A teacher can only make the effort of showing you truth, and prayerfully, inspire our hearts and minds to get better results than what we already have, or in the life of a student— we can only receive into our spirit-self what has been spiritually discerned and not much more. Please understand that information is not the same as revelation.

In information mode, one hears with their natural ear and sees with their natural eye and ponders with his natural intellect, but not much more than that. Now, believers, who walk by revelation are those who hear and see in the Spirit. In other words, their inner-man catches (catches being a selective word) a glimpse of the essence of God deep within. This can't be taught at the intellectual level or metaphysical level. Jesus told Nicodemus, **"Whatever is of the flesh is flesh and whatever is of the Spirit is Spirit!"** (see John 3 and read the discourse between Jesus and Nicodemus).

Here's what I have to say when it comes to getting more from the Lord: Listen to what the Spirit of the Lord within you is asking of you; listen carefully to the Spirit and do what He is asking you to do. Nothing brings more satisfaction and joy to the human heart than when one is aligned with God!

Time to Sit Under His Shadow and Learn!

1. Are you satisfied in your personal walk with God? Discuss this with your study group.

2. Do you believe that God has so much more for your life (career, work, ministry, family, economically, emotionally, physically, etc.)? Bounce this idea around with your group.

3. Have you ever felt lovesick for God? Share your experience with the group.

4. Information vs. Revelation. Can you describe the difference? Discuss these two words with the group.

5. Nothing brings more joy to the human heart than when we are obeying the Holy Spirit.

Day 30

The Life Which I Now Live!

"I have been crucified with Christ; it is no longer I who live, but Christ lives in me; and the life which I now live in the flesh I live by faith in the Son of God, who loved me and gave Himself for me." (Galatians 2:20)

When dealing with the Christian faith, many seem to take it very lightly. As a matter of fact, some call themselves Christians only because they like what Christianity stands for, the teachings of Jesus.

They like Christianity because it's a clean-cut lifestyle that promotes good values and principles— also, it brings about good conduct as its fruit.

I have spoken to people who love to hang around with Christian folk, because they are people who usually don't drink and are well-behaved. Though all this may be true, this is not true Christianity!

Let us look at Galatians 2:20 for a clear-cut definition of what it means to be a true Christian or at least the basis of what it entails to be one.

For starters, the Apostle Paul tells us of his very own Christian experience and how it all got started. He starts by saying, **"I have been crucified with Christ..."**.

In other words, Paul is saying that he personally took his life to the cross (not literally, but figuratively) to imitate Jesus. There must be a dying effect to self, if we are to ever understand what true Christianity is.

Paul continues his discourse and says, **"It is no longer I who live, but Christ lives in me."** .

As Paul died to himself (figuratively) he invites Christ to be the one living through him now. Do you see it?

An exchange has taken place. It is no longer Paul who lives, but instead Christ! The key here is that as the one coming into the kingdom of God yields his life to God— They experience the power of the Holy Spirit coming into dwell in themselves.

The life that one now lives must be a life of faith. As soon as Christ comes in, faith is activated so that a spirit-filled life can be lived out. The man or woman of faith will now be led to go to places where God will take him, say things God wants him to say, do things God may have him do, think and process the way God does, etc...

If you are a true Christian, then that means that you are led by the Spirit of God everywhere you go. You must be the judge if you are a true Christian or not.

Time to Sit Under His Shadow and Learn!

1. Are you a Christian? Why are you so sure? Share your experience with your study group.

2. Do you understand what Paul said when he says in Galatians 2:20, **"I am crucified with Christ and I no longer live, yet not I, but Christ lives in me?"** Discuss this concept with your group.

3. Have you begun to live a life of faith, or are you still waiting for something else to lead you along? Discuss with your group and share your own experience.

4. Do you find it hard to step out in faith and do God's will? Discuss with your group.

5. To be a true Christian, you must experience the cross of Christ. If you have not experienced dying to self, then you will have the hardest time walking with Christ. Share this thought with your group.

Day 31

The Deceit of Charm and Beauty!

"Charm is deceitful, and beauty is passing,
But a woman who fears the Lord, she shall be praised."
(Proverbs 31:30)

Charm and beauty are to a human being what a good paint job is to a car. People often become enamored with the external parts of the world, with little or perhaps no consideration of the internal. I think this way of seeing life will always exist in our world.

In the Proverb that I am breaking down for you, I felt like the Holy Spirit wanted me to share how easy people are attracted to outward things and how they set themselves up for failure by setting their affections on things of the earth. Is it any wonder why Paul said in Colossians 3:1, **"If then you were raised with Christ, seek those things which are above, where Christ is, sitting at the right hand of God. Set your mind on things above, not on things on the earth."**

The spiritual man always has with him an inclination toward spiritual things; it is easier for the spiritual man to discern the reality of things in comparison with the person who is caught up with externals.

Looking at the external is really not seeing things for what they really are. One must look past that, and discern with spiritual ability what God is really showing him or her.

Let us now look at this one verse in detail.

The writer of this Proverb says, **"Charm is deceitful, and beauty is passing".**

In other words, everything your eye is seeing, the charm and the beauty, it is all passing away. It is not here to stay with you or with anyone. In the same verse it says that **"charm is deceitful..."**

What you can see with your eyes is literally lying to you. It is lying to your five senses— however, it doesn't lie to the spiritual man who can discern!

The same Proverb states that **"beauty is passing."**

In other words, beauty will age. If we put our trust in beauty, we will be sadly disappointed! Do you see it?

Now the good news about this verse is that the comparison of beauty and charm does not even come close to someone who fears the Lord: **"But a woman who fears the Lord, she shall be praised."**

In dealing with the external, a woman's charm and beauty is quickly passing away, but if their hearts are in tune with God and she fears the Lord, she shall be praised.

Time to Sit Under His Shadow and Learn!

1. Charm and beauty are both deceitful and passing. Share with your study group on this subject and discuss it deeply. It is important to have a good perspective on internals and externals.

2. Have you ever fallen for externals, only to find out that they weren't right ? Share this with the group.

3. In Colossians 3:1, it exhorts us to not set our affections on things of the earth. What does this mean to you? Explain and share with the group.

4. Discernment is very important for every true believer to cultivate. How is your discernment on spiritual matters? Share with the group.

5. Learn to see behind the veil of the inauthentic external world. Don't buy into something right away; consult the Lord to see if this is what He has in store for you. Share this thought with your group and discuss.

Day 32

It is All Vanity!

**"Whatever my eyes desired I did not keep from them.
I did not withhold my heart from any pleasure,
For my heart rejoiced in all my labor;
And this was my reward from all my labor.
Then I looked on all the works that my hands had done
And on the labor in which I had toiled;
And indeed all was vanity and grasping for the wind.
There was no profit under the sun."** (Ecclesiastes 2:10, 11)

Have you ever read the book of Ecclesiastes? It's a must read for all who desire to know the intents of God's heart. Too often believers don't dive deep into the truths of God, and so missing the mark on what God's eternal word says, they miss out on God's eternal plan.

In these few verses, we have King Solomon unveiling, which in my opinion, has to be one of the most honest confessions I have ever heard. Most people don't want to open their hearts and share anything deep with others. feel embarrassed regarding attitudes that they have had, or decisions that they have made, decisions that led to heartbreak and even sorrow.

It is interesting to me that King Solomon was very honest about some of his deepest feelings, and we can learn from this.

He said that whatever his eyes desired, whatever his heart wanted, he didn't withhold any pleasurable thing away from them. He goes on to say that "his heart rejoiced in all his labor," and saw all the good things as rewards for all his heart work.

Unrestrained!

This is where I see many people today, enamored by materialism. Whatever they want they feel that they need to have! "After all," they say, "We are King's kids!" Have you ever fallen into such foolish thinking?

After this, King Solomon said,

"Then I looked on all the works that my hands had done

And on the labor in which I had toiled;
And indeed all was vanity and grasping for the wind.
There was no profit under the sun."

Isn't this the road that many have fallen into? Doesn't this sound a lot like us? We have the privilege of receiving something, (a blessing) and then we overindulge!

Eventually, this kind of lifestyle will get us to the place where we end-up compromising our convictions and end-up serving ourselves and not Jesus, the Lord!

In closing, King Solomon realized that it was all vanity and grasping for the wind. May the Lord open our eyes that we may see with His eyes!

Time to Sit Under His Shadow and Learn!

1. Living for Jesus must be lived with an open heart and mind before the Lord. Do you find yourself having a hard time doing this? Share with your study group.

2. When was the last time you had an experience with God, and the Holy Spirit really shook you to the core? Share your experience with your group.

3. King Solomon said that whatever his eyes desired, and whatever his heart desired, he never withheld anything from them. How does this sit with you? What are your thoughts on this? Share with the group.

4. The prosperity message that we hear in Christian circles today has to be one of the biggest misunderstandings being taught today. What is your view on prosperity? Share it with the group.

5. King Solomon came to a place in his life where he realized his error of overindulgence and said, **"Then I looked on all the works that my hands had done, and indeed all was vanity and grasping for the wind."** Do you feel like you need to, **"look on all the works of your hands,"** and evaluate your own life? Share with your group your thoughts on this.

Day 33

The Tudor!

"Therefore the law was our tutor to bring us to Christ, that we might be justified by faith. But after faith has come, we are no longer under a tutor." (Galatians 3:24, 25)

While mediating, praying, and fasting during my writing, I came to this passage which brings forth the subject of God's law. The law of God is good for us, it teaches us about what God wants and expects from His children and what He doesn't want as well.

Many have built doctrines over this topic, some have built curriculums, others have built churches based on this whole doctrine and some have even built whole denominations. Yes, whole denominations!

In the book of Acts, we saw this become an issue with the Judaizers. They felt that believers needed to, along with their faith in Christ, follow the law of Moses. This didn't sit well with the Apostle Paul, and he called them out for this erroneous teaching.

What is it about this teaching that brings about much controversy? Scholars and those who study apologetics, have all chimed in with their view on it, while others just followed suit, without even knowing why.

A Clear View

Now, the book of Galatians teaches us about the law of God. It specifically tells us that the law of God is our tutor to bring us to Christ. In the law of God, we find how wicked, selfish, and wayward, we are! It teaches us that we are sinners; it says that we are lost and undone without Christ.

The job of the law is to teach us how in need of God's forgiveness through Jesus Christ, we are. It brings us to attention and hopefully helps us realize how lost we are. Do you see this?

Once the law of God has done its job, it's up to us to repent of our sins by accepting Christ's free gift of salvation through his blood, which was shed at Calvary's cross. Let us keep the law of God ever before us— for it continually pushes us towards Jesus!

Time to Sit Under His Shadow and Learn!

1. Have you looked at the Law of God and discovered how imperfect you are? Nothing unveils our shortcomings like the Law of God. Please share with your study group if and how this resonates with you.

2. How many times have you evaluated your life by the Law of God and because of God's Law, you were able to find yourself back to the heart of God? Please share this with the group and discuss.

3. When you think of the word, tutor, what comes to your mind? Discuss this with the group.

4. The word tutor describes a person appointed to watch over a young child, train their public behavior, and keep them safe. Share this definition with the group and study it deeper.

5. Have you allowed the Law of God to be your tutor? Share with the group regarding your very own personal encounter with God's Law.

Day 34

Until Christ Is Formed!

"My little children, for whom I labor in birth again until Christ is formed in you..." (Galatians 4:19)

I want to thank the Lord for His mighty power and ever-increasing love towards me. The mercy that He has bestowed not only on me but on everyone who has made Him Savior and Lord! He has been faithful in so many ways, and I trust that He will continue to be there until the end of time.

When I think of the Lord, my heart melts with the desire to know Him. To understand His burning heart for me and how intensely He desires to show me His ways, His eternal ways, is unreal. I pray daily that these lovesick feelings I have for my King, will never subside for as long as I live here on earth.

Another thing I desire from the Lord is that my appetite for knowing Him, will always burn with intensity as well. I would rather die than lose the fire!

I Labor in Birth!

In reading the passage in Galatians 4:19, I had to pause for a bit and meditate deeper on what Paul was saying to these newly converted Galatians. Paul was obviously concerned for their spiritual well-being and didn't want any cult to come in and cheat them out of what Christ had given them.

He plainly told them that they needed to open their eyes and to not to be deceived by false teachings. It was only through Christ that they had found their salvation.

Paul took this personally. He felt like he was their spiritual father and needed to keep his watch over these young converts, **"until Christ would be formed in them."**

The work of helping people develop a strong spiritual life is never easy. As a matter of fact, I think it's one of the hardest things to do.

In the ministry of the Lord, one should always be conscious of the spiritual maturity of the freshly converted. We can't just leave them to figure the important things out. We must be intent in discipling them until they can stand on their own two feet.

Time to Sit Under His Shadow and Learn!

1. Do you experience God's daily love? Explain in what ways you have experienced this? Share with your study group.

2. What does being lovesick for God mean to you? Discuss this with the group.

3. Paul loved the Galatians. He was concerned over their relationship with God. He didn't want them to be led astray by Judaizers, or any other cult group that was teaching erroneous teachings. Are you aware of any false teachings that you have detected? Discuss with your group and share.

4. **"Until Christ be formed in you..."** What do these words mean to you? Please share with your group and discuss.

5. I believe that forming believers is the job of the church. The Holy Spirit will begin a deep work in them,

but the church must get them to the place where they can feed themselves!

Day 35

When the Honeymoon is Over!

**"The end of a thing is better than its beginning;
The patient in spirit is better than the proud in spirit."**
(Ecclesiastes 7:8)

I want to dive into this specific verse, as the Spirit of the Lord is moving me to write:

The end of a thing is better than its beginning, yes, but why? Most of us tend to praise those who jump into new ventures or new opportunities, supporting their every effort and wishing them well on their journey. I think we should always support those who release their God-given vision and talent.

In all this, we, who have been a bit more experienced in launching our projects, understand the honey-moon period. This is the period when emotions are high, things are on the up and up, and people are supporting us; it seems that everything is going great!

Up until this point, we still haven't woken-up to the reality of what awaits us as we navigate through our project. Then, suddenly without notice, without warning — the bottom falls off! Everything changes and we are left wondering.

Therefore, I believe that the end of a thing is better than the beginning, and here's why.

You see, as we begin our projects with great anticipation and excitement— the work of our hands will be tested. It will be tested to the very core. As we press through every adversity, our character is being molded and shaped, thus the Scripture line that follows is which says, "The patient in spirit is better than the proud in spirit."

There are two things that will manifest on our journey:

First, as we face adversity in our venture, our patience will be tested, or secondly, our fleshly pride will come forth!

Once again, our lives will be placed on display and the Lord will see it in full bloom. Do you understand what is happening here?

Just because we follow God with all our desire and lean upon the Lord with all our passion to serve him, it doesn't mean that we will be tested. Always remember that our lives are constantly under probation by the Spirit of the Lord.

Time to Sit Under His Shadow and Learn!

1. Do you know of someone who has ventured into a new project? What was your response to their new venture? Were you supportive? Share with your study group and discuss.

2. Knowing that many tests and trials await those who venture into new endeavors, support them the best way you can through prayer and encouraging words.

3. Anyone who believes that they should take steps to open a ministry, a business, or start a family, must always count the cost. The cost is expensive! Be wise and plan your future the best way you can. Discuss this point with your group and share your own vision and heart.

4. In your own words, describe what "The end of a thing is better than its beginning" means to you? Share

your definition with your group.

5. The Scripture says that through patience they inherited the promises. Though the journey may seem long, it will come to an end. Keep walking forward!

Day 36

It Will Be Well!

"Though a sinner does evil a hundred times, and his days are prolonged, yet I surely know that it will be well with those who fear God, who fear before Him. But it will not be well with the wicked; nor will he prolong his days, which are as a shadow, because he does not fear before God." (Ecclesiastes 8:12, 13)

I have been meditating upon this one verse and it is truly an amazing way of thinking when it comes down to judging sinners.

I think too often, we think that lost sinners (people who don't know Jesus as Lord and Savior yet) seem to get away with all the sins they commit. It almost seems that God doesn't look at all their wrong-doing or simply, ignores their foolishness.

Looking from the outside in, it appears that lost sinners go unpunished for some of the most heinous crimes committed against people and against God! "It's not fair," I have heard some say.

We might even think that they are getting away with such injustice and there is no one to defend our cause. Yet, this couldn't be further from the truth!

In Ecclesiastes, the writer King Solomon bears out an awesome truth. He says, **"yet I surely know that it will be well with those who fear God…".**

In essence, King Solomon is saying, Look, I know that it seems like sinners get away with a whole bunch. I don't know how much, but I know they do. The honest truth is that I don't really concern myself with how many times they get away with sin, but one thing I do know: I surely know that it will be well with those who fear God!

Instead of allowing ourselves to get bitter and angry because of evildoers, we should pray for God's mercy upon them—suffice to know that there are some rough days coming to them, in a very short while. Listen to what the Scripture says, **"But it will not be well with the wicked; nor will he prolong his days, which are as a shadow."**

In not fearing the Lord, the lost sinner sets themselves up for failure. They will destroy their blessings in their own generation and who knows if the next generation will survive the previous generation?

Time to Sit Under His Shadow and Learn!

1. Have you ever felt like lost sinners get away with their sin? Share with your study group.

2. Have you ever wondered when punishment is coming their way? What was your attitude? Share what you have learned from this emotion.

3. "Fearing the Lord" means what to you? Explain and share your definition with the group.

4. Those who fear the Lord, things go well for them. Those who don't fear the Lord, eventually, all hell will break loose upon them! Have you experienced this in your own life? Share your story with the group.

5. The fear of the Lord is the beginning of wisdom. With all you have within you, give yourself to the fear of the Lord. Learn to revere Him in all things! Share

the thought with your group.

Day 37

With All Your Might!

"Whatever your hand finds to do, do it with your might; for there is no work or device or knowledge or wisdom in the grave where you are going." (Ecclesiastes 9:10)

What an awesome universal principle this is! Whatever your hand finds to do, do it with your might. I think that once we understand the depth of this one particular principle, it will transform our thinking in how we do our daily chores.

I often hear teenagers say, I am bored!

Why are they bored? What is it about their surroundings that they don't like? What is it that makes them hate their present situation? Is life really that boring? Or is that they just don't have a vision for it yet?

It is hard to do anything with all your might, when you have nothing to do!

I have seen the same attitude in adults. They are bored out of their minds, and feel that their lives are going nowhere fast. They work, they have a family, they go to church, but they don't have a bigger picture of life altogether. Some of these servants of God only do what they are expected to do, but not much more than that!

When people are looking for promotions, they usually don't know why they need one, apart from the idea that it will make them more money. It's truly a sad place to be in the Lord— not knowing what God has in store for you.

In the Flesh!

In the flesh, or in the power of the soul, many have accomplished great things. They have done great exploits for their companies, for their families, and even in some type of religious setting.

If you did what you did with all your might, good. You will get your just reward by those who you did it for.

Eternal View!

Now, if you did with your hand the will of the Lord, and you did it with all your might, can you imagine what God did with what you offered Him. If you did what you did with an eternal value in mind, how great the dividends of that investment would be!

Time to Sit Under His Shadow and Learn!

1. Do you have a vision for your life? If you do, share it with your study group and discuss.

2. In persevering for more of God in your life, do you do it with all your might, or do you do it when it's convenient for you? Share it with the group.

3. In the flesh or soul, we can all look good in front of people and for the glory of people. Actually, it is the people who will give us our reward. Review this point and share with your group.

4. Have you developed this work ethic? The ethic of working for others with all your might? Share with the group.

5. We only live once! If we don't do it, then who will? If not now, then when? Meditate upon these words and discuss them as a group.

Day 38

Recognize Yourself!

**"If the ax is dull,
And one does not sharpen the edge,
Then he must use more strength;
But wisdom brings success."** (Ecclesiastes 10:10)

In this prophet word, I heard the Lord say to me, "David, you must always recognize yourself."

I wasn't too sure what the Lord meant by this so I asked again, and He clarified in the most awesome of ways! Let me share this with you.

When someone is full of themselves, as we say of people who are arrogant and proud and have a big ego— it is very difficult for that individual to see any wrong in their attitude, in their way of thinking, in their actions, and in their overview of life.

People that are full of themselves don't see the world from

a realistic perspective. Now, they do have knowledge, the only problem is, it's knowledge without wisdom! In other words, they know a lot, but they don't know when share it. Most of these people don't know when to shut up, they don't realize when they have offended someone, and they don't have a clue when to slow down or go faster on a matter! And these my friends, are people, who don't recognize themselves!

Let me share with you a bit about this verse and why I believe it speaks to our very subject right now.

The Scripture reads, **"The ax is dull, and one does not sharpen the edge."**

What this means is that those who are full of themselves, those who don't recognize the facts, keep hammering away until they burn-out and quit in life altogether. They will eventually quit their pursuit of health, their pursuit of good relationships, their ambition for promotion— yes, they will quit their job, their marriage, and finally quit on their faith in Christ!

When one is burnt-out due to using a lot of strength due to a dull axe, one eventually stops fighting for what he believes.

Be watchful and learn to recognize yourself.

Lastly, the Scripture closes by saying, **"But wisdom brings success."**

This is a no-brainer. Anyone who sets themselves to ponder and look will recognize what needs to be done to be successful. Take some time to make all the necessary changes, arrangements and position yourself for success. Success doesn't happen automatically; it only happens to those who know how to read the signs of the times!

Time to Sit Under His Shadow and Learn!

The words, full of themselves, what do they mean to you? Discuss it with your study group.

Have you been guilty of being full of yourself? This is a time to come clean with your group and share your heart on the matter. Listen as others share theirs as well.

The Scripture reads: **"The ax is dull, and one does not sharpen the edge."** What does this mean to you? Explain and share with the group.

Have you experienced a dull ax while trying to get something done and it just wasn't working out for you? Share this.

Wisdom brings success is a set of powerful words. Find the wisdom in everything you read, study, and write. It will be rewarding in the long haul. Share these thoughts with your group.

Day 39

Learning to Sow Continually!

"In the morning sow your seed,
And in the evening do not withhold your hand;
For you do not know which will prosper,
Either this or that,
Or whether both alike will be good." (Ecclesiastes 11:6)

In life, I have come to know that unless you are pressing forward, you will be going backwards. Not that we desire to go backwards, but just like gravity, our lives will gravitate backwards by the simple nature of living in this world.

This is the reason why people are always challenging us to keep moving forward. You might even hear some of the trainers at a local gym say, You can do it! Don't give up! One more time!

Why all the pushing and pressing to go deeper, faster, and go longer! Because in all labor there is profit. **"In all hard**

work there is profit, but the talk of the lips leads only to poverty." (Proverbs 14:23)

If you keep pressing forward, eventually, something good will come out of it! This is the idea.

I have also discovered that a winner's attitude is based on these wise words. People who are champions in life and winners in most areas (relationship, finances, spiritual life, emotional life, career, vocation, or business life, etc.) of their lives practice these principles.

They understand that to be able to get from point A to point B, action must be taken not only once, but countless times. Risk, effort, and hard work are needed to get the breakthroughs that we are seeking!

The Scripture says that in the morning and in the evening, sowing must take place. Don't just do it once, but numerous times. Why? Because we don't know when the seeds will sprout, or which ones will eventually bear fruit.

Don't only be a winner in life, be a student of life as well. Learn to give until you have nothing more to give!
Time to Sit Under His Shadow and Learn!

Working hard is truly an invitation to success. The man who talks and does nothing— gets nothing! Discuss this viewpoint with your study group.

The Scripture says that in all labor there is profit. What does this Scripture mean to you? Share your understanding with your group.

Often people tend to give up when they don't see any fruit coming forth. There is a reason why people do this. Don't let this be you! Learn to press in until you see the new shoots come forth! Share with your group.

One of the things that we must learn to do as God's servants, is to be creative with our God-given gifts. The Lord may call you to serve Him in one way or the other. Take time to discover the many ways you can accomplish God's will. Share with the group your thoughts and ask around to see what they think.

Learn to sow continually. You will not regret it! Reflect on this thought as a group.

Day 40

Man's Initial Calling!

**"Let us hear the conclusion of the whole matter:
Fear God and keep His commandments,
For this is man's all."** (Ecclesiastes 12:13)

Of all the things we can speak of in our understanding of God, and the myriad of spiritual subjects we can read and study, nothing is more valuable than to grasp what is truly important to God's heart— to fear Him and to keep His commandments!

In the place where God has brought me to in my short walk with Him, I have learned a thing or two about doing the things that please Him; I also have learned and have firmly grasped a hold of the things that don't please Him!

In this journey with the Spirit of God leading me, I have also known temptation, sin, struggle, fear, doubt, and have succumbed to many of these things; however, in His mercy and ever-increasing love for me, I have found my way out from the abyss!

I have learned to walk in the Spirit, but I have also given way to the flesh. I have followed my carnal desires once too many times, but I have also learned to lay my life down for the sake of the call. Many times, I have whined, cried, and complained, yet many times I have run to the mercy-seat and found help during my time of need!

I say all this to say that in God's awesome plan, life can be lived to the fullest potential, if one will give themselves to the fear of the Lord and to embrace His commandments and do them!

"To fear God and do His commandments is man's all," said King Solomon.

Should we take advice from this man who experienced riches, wisdom, and wealth? We would be wise to take counsel from him! Nothing can teach us more powerfully, then a man who tasted it all, and found it to be nothing but vanity. In the lateral part of his life, King Solomon, in essence was saying, Look! I have done it all, have had it all, and as nice as outward things are, they are vanity in the clock of eternity! Don't fall for the stuff, rather fear God and just obey Him in all His ways!

Time to Sit Under His Shadow and Learn!

1. The Scripture says that fearing God and keeping His commands is man's all. What is your take upon reading these powerful words? Share with your study group what this means to you.

2. What is your definition of "fearing God?" What does it mean to you to fear God? Discuss this with your group.

3. What other subjects have you studied in your Bible that you think are also of great value? Share with the group.

4. Evaluating our lives on a regular basis is not only important but it is also healthy. When was the last time you did an honest evaluation of yourself? Share your thoughts with your group.

5. King Solomon is the portrait of a man who was wise and prosperous. He was the richest king that ever

lived in his day and experienced much under the sun. Though he had everything, he became blinded by his success. Take his life as a warning and learn to stay steadfast in God. There will be many challenges, but fear God and do His commandments— if you do, you will reap the benefits of a righteous life!

Ministry Resources

Most Shabar Publications products are available at special quantity discounts for bulk purchase for sales promotions, fund-raising and educational needs. For details, write Shabar Publications at mayorga1126@gmail.com.

For the purchase of more books
written by David Mayorga,
visit our bookstore at:

www.shabarpublications.com

Ministry Information

Shabar Publications is a ministry expression under Masterbuilder Ministries, Inc. in Palmhurst, Texas. This publication ministry, was founded and created for the purpose of writing books and distributing them to the body of Christ both locally and globally. The intent behind the idea of publishing these works, is to train and equip the reader to be a more intimate lover of Jesus Christ, our Lord! Out of an intimate life with God, by the grace of God, effective ministry will be the outflow.

For more information regarding this ministry, feel free to email us at: mayorga1126@gmail.com.

www.ingramcontent.com/pod-product-compliance
Lightning Source LLC
Chambersburg PA
CBHW071448070526
44578CB00001B/254